G000123968

GRANDMA'S FAVOURITES

PIES & TARTS

MARGARET KEENAN

T&J

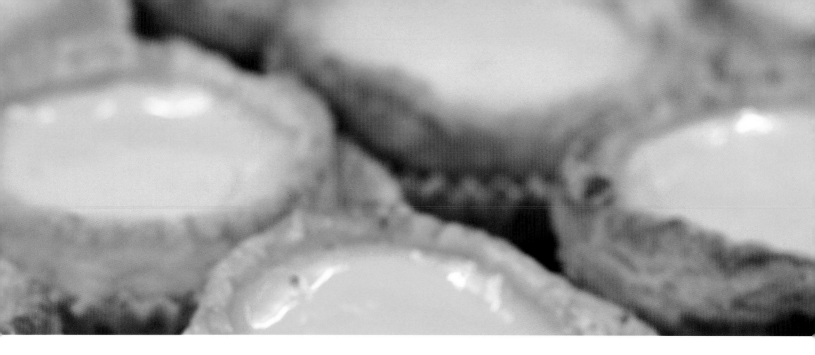

Published in 2010 by TAJ Books International LLP

27, Ferndown Gardens,
Cobham,
Surrey,
UK,
KT11 2BH

www.tajbooks.com

Copyright ©2010 Taj Books International LLP

Copyright under International, Pan American, and Universal Copyright Conventions. All rights reserved.
No part of this book may be reproduced or transmitted in any form or by any means, electronic or mechanical,
including photocopying, recording, or by any information storage-and-retrieval system, without written permission
from the copyright holder. Brief passages (not to exceed 1,000 words) may be quoted for reviews.

All notations of errors or omissions (author inquiries, permissions) concerning the content of this book
should be addressed to TAJ Books 27, Ferndown Gardens, Cobham, Surrey, UK, KT11 2BH, info@tajbooks.com.

ISBN-13: 978-1-84406-165-5

Printed in China.

CONTENTS

APPLE LATTICE PIE

Metric	Ingredient	Imperial
	(for the filling)	
690 g	thinly sliced peeled apples	5 1/2 cups
200 g	sugar	1 cup
	2 tbsp water	
	4 1/2 tsp quick-cooking tapioca	
	1/2 tsp ground cinnamon	
	1/4 tsp ground nutmeg	
	(for the pastry)	
250 g	all-purpose flour	2 cups
	1/2 tsp baking powder	
	1/2 tsp salt	
135 g	shortening	2/3 cup
	5 tbsp cold water	
	3 tbsp butter	
	2 tbsp milk	
	1 tbsp sugar	

Method

1. **In a large bowl,** combine the apples, sugar, water, tapioca, cinnamon and nutmeg; toss to coat. Let stand for 15 minutes.

2. **In a large bowl,** combine the flour, baking powder and salt; cut in shortening until crumbly. Gradually add water, tossing with a fork until dough forms a ball. Divide in half, making one half slightly larger.

3. **On a lightly floured** surface, roll out larger portion of pastry to fit a 9-in. pie plate. Transfer pastry to plate; trim even with edge of plate. Add filling; dot with butter. Roll out remaining pastry; make a lattice crust. Trim, seal and flute edges.

4. **Brush with milk; sprinkle** with sugar. Cover edges loosely with foil.

5. **Bake at 200 ° C/400 ° F/Gas Mark 6** for 15 minutes. Reduce heat to 180 ° C/350 ° F/Gas Mark 4; bake 40-50 minutes longer or until crust is golden brown and filling is bubbly. Cool on a wire rack.

APPLE PIE

Metric	Ingredient	Imperial
	(for the filling)	
150 g	white sugar	3/4 cup
	2 tbsp all-purpose flour	
	1/2 tsp ground cinnamon	
	1/4 tsp ground nutmeg	
	1/2 tsp lemon zest	
875 g	thinly sliced apples	7 cups
	2 tsp lemon juice	
	1 tbsp butter	
	4 tbsp milk	
	(for the pastry)	
250 g	all-purpose flour	2 cups
	1/2 tsp baking powder	
	1/2 tsp salt	
135 g	shortening	2/3 cup
	5 tbsp cold water	
	3 tbsp butter	
	2 tbsp milk	
	1 tbsp sugar	

Method

1. **In a large bowl,** combine the flour, baking powder and salt; cut in shortening until crumbly. Gradually add water, tossing with a fork until dough forms a ball. Divide in half, making one half slightly larger.

2. **On a lightly floured** surface, roll out larger portion of pastry to fit a 9-in. pie plate. Transfer pastry to plate; trim even with edge of plate. Add filling; dot with butter. Roll out remaining pastry.

3. **Preheat oven to** 220 ° C/425 ° F/Gas Mark 7. Mix together the sugar, flour, cinnamon, nutmeg and lemon peel.

4. **Place second pie crust** on top of filling and flute the edges. Cut vents in top crust and brush with milk for a glazed appearance if desired. Bake for 40 to 50 minutes.

APRICOT AND ALMOND TART

Metric	Ingredient	Imperial
375 g	packet dessert shortcrust pastry	13 oz
	1 medium egg, plus 1 medium egg yolk	
50 g	unsalted butter, melted	2 oz
100 g	golden caster sugar, plus an extra 1 tbsp	4 oz
100 g	ground almonds	4 oz
	1 tbsp amaretto or brandy	
	8 fresh apricots, halved and stoned	
	23cm loose bottomed flan tin	

Method

1. **Preheat the oven to** 200 ° C/400 ° F/Gas Mark 6. Place a baking sheet in the oven to heat.

2. **On a floured surface** roll out the pastry and use to line the flan tin.

3. **In a bowl, mix** together the egg, egg yolk, butter, caster sugar, ground almonds and amaretto or brandy.

4. **Spoon the mixture into** the base of the flan case.

5. **Arrange the apricots, cut** side up on the almond paste.

6. **Sprinkle with the extra** caster sugar and place the flan on the preheated baking tray.

7. **Bake for 30 -** 35 minutes or until firm and golden brown.

8. **Serve warm or at** room temperature.

APRICOT TART

Metric	Ingredient	Imperial	Metric	Ingredient	Imperial
	(for the Short Crust Pastry)			(for the filling)	
350 g	all-purpose flour	2 1/2 cups	454 g	fresh apricots, cut into 1/2 inch (1.5 cm) pieces	2 lb
	1 tsp salt			3 tbsp cornstarch	
	2 tbsp granulated white sugar		150 g	granulated white sugar	3/4 cup
226 g	unsalted butter, chilled, and cut into 1 inch (2.54 cm) chunks	1 cup		1/4 tsp ground cinnamon	
				1 tsp fresh lemon juice	
60 - 120 ml	ice water	1/4 to 1/2 cup		2 tbsp unsalted butter, cut into small chunks	

Method

1. **Make the pastry: In** a food processor, place the flour, salt, and sugar and process until combined. Add the butter and process. Pour 1/4 cup (60 ml) water in a steady stream, until the dough just holds together when pinched. Turn the dough onto your work surface and gather into a ball. Divide the dough in half, flattening each half into a disk, cover with plastic wrap, and refrigerate for about one hour before using.

2. **Remove one portion of** the dough and place it on a lightly floured surface. Roll the pastry into a 12 inch (30 cm) circle. Fold the dough in half and gently transfer to a 9 inch (23 cm) pie pan. Refrigerate the pastry, covered with plastic wrap.

3. **Remove the second round** of pastry and roll it into a 13 inch (30 cm) circle. Using a pastry wheel, cut the pastry into 3/4 inch (2 cm) strips. Place the strips of pastry on a parchment paper-lined baking sheet, cover with plastic wrap, and place in the refrigerator for about 10 minutes. Preheat the oven to 200 ° C/400 °F/Gas Mark 6.

4. **Now make the filling:** Place the apricots in a large bowl. In a small bowl mix together the cornstarch, sugar, and ground cinnamon. Remove the chilled pie crust from the fridge. Sprinkle about 2 tablespoons of the sugar mixture over the pastry crust. Add the remaining sugar mixture to the apricots and gently toss to combine. Pour the fruit mixture into the prepared pie shell. Sprinkle the fruit with about 1 teaspoon of lemon juice and dot with 2 tablespoons of butter.

5. **Remove the lattice pastry** from the refrigerator and, starting at the center with the longest strips and working outwards, space the strips about 3/4 inch (2 cm) apart. Then, rotate pie plate a quarter turn, and repeat the process with the rest of the strips. Weave the top strips over and under the bottom strips. Seal the by folding them under the bottom pastry crust. Place the pie plate on the hot baking sheet and bake the pie for about 45 minutes until the crust is a golden brown color and the fruit juices begin to bubble.

6. **Remove the pie from** the oven and place on a wire rack to cool for several hours.

BAKEWELL TART

Metric	Ingredient	Imperial
	(for the pastry)	
50 g	butter or margarine	2 oz
100 g	plain (all-purpose) flour	4 oz
	2 tbsp water	
	(for the filling)	
100 g	strawberry jam	4 oz
50 g	butter or margarine, softened	2 oz
50 g	caster (superfine) sugar	2 oz
	1 egg, lightly beaten	
	A few drops of almond essence (extract)	
25 g	self-raising (self-rising) flour	1 oz
25 g	ground almonds	1 oz
50 g	flaked (slivered) almonds	2 oz

Method

1. **To make the pastry,** rub the butter or margarine into the flour until the mixture resembles breadcrumbs.

2. **Stir in just enough** water to mix to a pastry. Roll out and use to line a greased 18 cm/7 in flan tin.

3. **Spread with the jam.** To make the filling, cream together the butter or margarine and sugar, then beat in the egg and almond essence.

4. **Stir in the flour** and ground almonds. Spoon over the jam and level the surface. Sprinkle with the flaked almonds.

5. **Bake in a preheated** oven at 190 ° C/375 ° F/Gas Mark 5 for 20 minutes.

BANOFFEE PIE

Metric	Ingredient	Imperial
300 g	oaty biscuits (Hob Nobs are good)	10 1/2 oz
60 g	butter, melted	2 oz
397 g	tin Nestlé Carnation Caramel	14 oz
	3 large bananas , sliced	
350 ml	double cream	12 fl oz
	1 tbsp icing sugar	
100 g	dark chocolate	3 1/2 oz

Method

1. Heat the oven to 180 ° C/350 ° F/Gas Mark 4.

2. Crush the biscuits in a food processor then add the melted butter and pulse to combine. Press the mixture into a 24cm tart tin, with a removable base, in an even layer.

3. Transfer the tin to a baking sheet and cook for 10-12 minutes, until lightly toasted and set. Leave to cool then gently release from the tin and put on a serving plate.

4. Spread the caramel over the biscuit base and chill for 1 hour. Arrange the banana slices over the toffee. Whip the cream and sugar together to form soft peaks and spread over the bananas. melt the chocolate in a microwave or in a bowl set over, not in, a pan of simmering water.

5. Allow to cool slightly, before drizzling over the cream.

BLUEBERRY PIE

Metric	Ingredient	Imperial
	2 tbsp butter	
115 g	brown sugar, firmly packed	1 cup
	1 can blueberries, drained, reserve liquid	
	3 egg yolks, beaten	
115 g	granulated sugar	1 cup
115 g	all-purpose flour	1 cup
	1 tsp baking powder	
	1 tsp salt	
	3 egg whites, beaten until stiff peaks form	

Method

1. **In a saucepan, combine** butter, brown sugar, and 1/2 cup of the juice from canned blueberries. Cook until sugar is dissolved.

2. **Cover bottom of a** buttered 9-inch square baking pan with the drained blueberries; pour cooked syrup over them.

3. **In a mixing bowl,** beat together the egg yolks, granulated sugar, and 5 more tablespoons of the blueberry liquid.

4. **Sift together the flour,** baking powder, and salt; stir into the egg yolk mixture. Fold in egg whites.

5. **Pour batter over the** blueberries in baking dish. Bake in a preheated 180 ° C/350 ° F/Gas Mark 4 oven for 45 minutes.

6. **Remove cake from oven;** immediately run spatula around edge of pan and invert onto a serving plate. Before lifting the pan off, let syrup drain onto the cake for a few minutes.

7. **Cut while still warm;** top each serving with whipped cream, if desired.

BLUEBERRY TART

Metric	Ingredient	Imperial
	(for the crust)	
115 g	flour	1 cup
	1/4 tsp salt	
	2 tbsp sugar	
57 g	butter, cold	1/2 cup
	1 tbsp white vinegar	
	(for the filling)	
115 g	sugar	1 cup
	2 tbsp flour	
	1/8 tsp cinnamon	
520 g	blueberries, divided	4 1/2 cups

Method

1. **Preheat oven to 200** ° C/400°F/Gas Mark 6 and spray 10-inch springform pan with non-stick cooking spray. Combine flour, salt and sugar.

2. **Cut in the butter** with pastry blender or fork and mix in the vinegar.

3. **Pat crust onto bottom** of springform pan and 1 inch up side.

4. **For the filling combine** sugar, flour and cinnamon. Add 2 1/2 cups blueberries and place evenly on top of crust.

5. **Bake for 1 hour** and remove from the oven and put remaining 2 cups blueberries on top, lightly pressing in blueberries. **Cool completely.**

6. **Remove rim and serve** from springform bottom.

BLUEBERRY TARTLETS

Metric	Ingredient	Imperial
	1 1/2 sheets short-crust pastry	
150 g	white chocolate	5 oz
43 g	cream	1 1/2 oz
250 g	fresh blueberries	9 oz
	icing sugar	

Method

1. **Preheat oven 180 ° C/350 ° F/Gas Mark 4,** spray patty pan tray with oil. Cut 12 x 7 cm rounds in pastry, ease into pan, chill for 30 mins.

2. **Cut 12 x 8** cm circles from non stick baking paper, line tray with these circles, put pastry on top, with dried beans for weighting. bake for 10 mins. Remove paper, beans. and bake for another 5 mins.

3. **Allow to cool. Place** chocolate, cream over saucepan, and melt. (ensure the base of bowl doesn't touch simmering water). Pour into pastry cases once smooth. refrigerate for 1 hour.

4. **Top with blueberries and** dust with icing sugar

CALZONE

Metric	Ingredient	Imperial
	(for the dough)	
225 g	plain strong flour, plus extra for dusting	8 oz
90 ml	milk, warmed to body temperature	3 fl oz
50 ml	water, warmed to body temperature	2 fl oz
	1 tsp dried yeast	
25 ml	olive oil	1 fl oz
	pinch salt	
	(for the filling)	
150 g	cherry tomatoes, halved	5 oz
200 g	buffalo mozzarella, roughly chopped	7 oz
200 g	assorted Italian cold meats (for example: salami, prosciutto, speck)	7 oz
	1 tbsp capers, rinsed and drained	
30 g	grated parmesan	1 oz

Method

1. **Preheat the oven to** 230 ° C/450 ° F/Gas Mark 8. Place a baking tray into the oven to preheat.

2. **For the dough, sift** the flour into a bowl. Mix the milk, water and yeast together in a separate bowl. Add the yeast mixture to the flour and mix together to form a dough. Knead the dough for five minutes on a floured and even service. Add the olive oil and knead again to combine. Cover the bowl with cling film and leave somewhere warm for two hours. Add the salt to the dough and knead again, then divide the dough into four equal portions and roll into balls.

4. **Place each ball onto** a floured work surface and roll out into 20cm/8in circles.

5. **For the filling, place** all of the filling ingredients into a bowl and mix together well. Place one quarter of the filling mixture onto one half of each dough circle, leaving a 2cm/1in gap around the edge.

6. **Brush the clean edges** with water then fold the other sides over to cover the filling and pinch the edges to seal the four parcels.

7. **Place the calzones onto the** preheated baking sheet and transfer to the oven to bake for eight minutes, or until the dough is cooked through and the filling hot.

CHANTERLLE MUSHROOM AND BLUE CHEESE PIE

Metric	Ingredient	Imperial
	puff pastry (about 4 sheets if using squares)	
200 g	chanterelle mushrooms	7oz
100 g	Blue cheese	3 1/2 oz
50 g	Pecorino grated	2
	1 pcs egg for eggwash	
	1/2 tbsp olive oil	

Method

1. **Preheat the oven to** 225 ° C/110 ° F/Gas Mark 1/4.

2. **Cut the chanterelles into** manageable sizes. Keep in mind it needs to fit on top of the puff pastry and you don't want huge chunks here but not too small either. In a bowl toss the mushrooms with olive oil and salt and pepper to taste.

3. **Take the puff pastry** (defrosted ofcourse) and put some of the mushrooms in the middle, making sure to leave the sides free. Don't be too shy; you want to have a nice little pile of mushrooms there. They will decrease in size in the oven.

4. **Generously add little chunks** of the blue cheese here and there. Make sure to have an even distribution of cheesy goodness there. Once done sprinkle the grated pecorino on top.

5. **Put some eggwash on** the sides of the puff pastry and fold it creatively in a little basket, so that the cheese stays in when it starts to melt. Plus the corners will become nice and crispy too. Pinch it tightly to make sure it stays put once heated.

6. **Put the little pies** in the oven for about 12 minutes on high, then bring the temperature down to 190 °C and bake for another 15 minutes until golden brown and crispy.

CHEESE PIE

Metric	Ingredient	Imperial
200 g	flaky pastry	8 oz
200 g	grated cheese	8 oz
	1 egg, beaten	
	2 onions, chopped finely	

Method

1. **Roll out the pastry** and line a flan tin. Reserve enough for a lid.

2. **Cook the onions in** boiling water for 5 minutes.

3. **Make sure they are** well drained, add nearly all the egg and season.

4. **Mix with the cheese.** Pour the cheese and onion mixture into the pie.

5. **Damp the edges of** the pastry in the dish and fit a lid on top.

6. **Press the edges well** together and decorate.

7. **Brush to glaze with** the remaining egg.

8. **Bake in the top** of a 200 ° C/400 ° F/Gas Mark 6 oven for 30 minutes.

CHICKEN PIE

Metric	Ingredient	Imperial
	1 packet ready roll pastry	
60 g	butter	2 oz
	1 small onion, minced	
	2 sticks celery, chopped	
	2 carrots, diced	
	salt and pepper to taste	
	2 chicken stock	
500 ml	water	17 fl oz
	3 potatoes, peeled and cubed	
225 g	cooked chicken, cubed	8 oz
	3 tablespoons plain flour	
125 ml	full fat milk	4 fl oz
	3 tablespoons chopped fresh parsley	
	1 teaspoon chopped fresh oregano	

Method

1. **Preheat oven to 220** ° C/425 ° F/Gas Mark 7. Roll out one piece of pastry and place in a 20cm pie dish and set aside.

2. **Place 1/2 of the** butter in a large frying pan. Add the onion, celery, carrots, salt and pepper. Cook and stir until the vegetables are soft. Stir in the stock cubes and water. Bring mixture to the boil. Stir in the potatoes, and cook until tender but still firm.

3. **In a medium saucepan,** melt the remaining butter. Stir in the chicken and flour. Add the milk, and heat through. Stir the turkey mixture into the vegetable mixture, and cook until thickened. Add fresh herbs. Pour mixture into the unbaked pastry case. Roll out the top piece of pastry, and place on top of filling. Flute edges, and make 4 slits in the top to let out steam.

4. **Bake in the preheated** oven for 15 minutes. Reduce oven temperature to 180 ° C/350 ° F/Gas Mark 4 and continue baking for 20 minutes, or until pastry is golden brown.

CHICKEN POT PIE

Metric	Ingredient	Imperial
455 g	skinless, boneless chicken breast halves - cubed	1 lb
120 g	sliced carrots	1 cup
150 g	frozen green peas	1 cup
60 g	sliced celery	1/2 cup
75 g	butter	1/3 cup
55 g	chopped onion	1/3 cup
40 g	all-purpose flour	1/3 cup
	1/2 tsp salt	
	1/4 tsp black pepper	
	1/4 tsp celery seed	
415 ml	chicken broth	
160 ml	milk	
	2 (9 inch) unbaked pie crusts	

Method

1. **Preheat oven to** 220 ° C/425 ° F/Gas Mark 7.

2. **In a saucepan, combine** chicken, carrots, peas, and celery. Add water to cover and boil for 15 minutes. Remove from heat, drain and set aside.

3. **In the saucepan over** medium heat, cook onions in butter until soft and translucent. Stir in flour, salt, pepper, and celery seed. Slowly stir in chicken broth and milk. Simmer over medium-low heat until thick. Remove from heat and set aside.

4. **Place the chicken mixture** in bottom pie crust. Pour hot liquid mixture over. Cover with top crust, seal edges, and cut away excess dough. Make several small slits in the top to allow steam to escape.

5. **Bake in the preheated** oven for 30 to 35 minutes, or until pastry is golden brown and filling is bubbly. Cool for 10 minutes before serving.

CHOCOLATE AND CARAMEL TART

Metric	Ingredient	Imperial
	(for the crust)	
115 g	all purpose flour	1 cup
	3 tbsp sugar	
	1 tsp grated lemon peel	
	1/8 tsp salt	
57 g	unsalted butter, cut into 1/2-inch pieces	1/2 cup
	1 large egg yolk	
	1/2 tsp vanilla extract	
	(for chocolate filling)	
90 g	whipping cream	3/4 cup
	bittersweet (not unsweetened) or semisweet chocolate, finely chopped	6 oz
	(for caramel filling)	
90 g	sugar	3/4 cup
35 g	water	1/3 cup
35 g	whipping cream	1/3 cup
	5 tbsp unsalted butter	
	1/2 tsp vanilla extract	

Method

1. **Blend the crust ingredients** and process until large moist clumps form. Gather dough into ball. Flatten into disk. Wrap in plastic; chill until firm enough to roll.

2. **Preheat oven to 200 ° C/400 ° F/Gas Mark 6.** Roll out dough between sheets of plastic wrap to 12-inch round. Peel off plastic. Turn dough over; press into 9-inch-diameter tart pan with removable bottom. Fold in any excess dough, forming double-thick sides. Freeze 15 minutes. Bake crust 10 minutes. Using back side of fork, press crust flat if bottom bubbles. continue to bake until crust is golden, about 10 minutes.

4. **Bring cream to boil** in heavy small saucepan and whisk until smooth. Spread 1 cup chocolate filling in prepared crust. Refrigerate until firm, about 45 minutes. reserve remaining filling in saucepan.

5. **stir sugar and a** 1/3 of the water in heavy medium saucepan over low heat until sugar dissolves. Increase heat and boil until syrup is amber color, brushing down sides with wet pastry brush, about 8 minutes. Remove from heat. Add the rest of the ingredients. Return pan to very low heat; stir until caramel is smooth and color deepens. Refrigerate for about 20 minutes. Spoon caramel filling over chocolate filling. Pipe of drizzle reserved chocolate filling decoratively over cararmel (if chocolate is too firm to pour, warm slightly over low heat). Refrigerate tart until caramel is firm, at least 1 hour. (Can be made 2 days ahead. Cover keep chilled.)

CREAM CHEESE AND CUCUMBER TART

Metric	Ingredient	Imperial
	butter, softened	1/2 cup
	all-purpose flour	1 cup
	cream cheese, softened	3 oz
	1 large cucumber, skinned and chopped	
	parsely to garnish	

Method

1. **Mix butter and flour** just until blended. Chill about 1 hour. This can be made ahead and chilled for up to 24 hours.

2. **Preheat oven to 170** ° C/325 ° F/Gas Mark 3.

3. **Shape dough into 24** one-inch balls and press into ungreased 1 1/2 inch muffin cups (mini-muffin size) to make a shallow shell.

4. **Mix the cream cheese** and the chopped cucumber together.

5. **Spoon the mixture into** the shells.

6. **Garnish with the parsley** and serve.

CUSTARD TART

Metric	Ingredient	Imperial
	(for the pastry)	
250 g	plain flour	9 oz
100 g	unsalted butter	4 1/2 oz
	2 eggs	
100 g	icing sugar	4 1/2 oz
	4 drops vanilla extract	
	(for the custard)	
480 ml	whipping cream	16 fl oz
	6 egg yolks	
70 g	caster sugar	2 1/2 oz
	1 vanilla pod, split	
	grated nutmeg	

Method

1. **Pre-heat oven to 180** ° C/350 ° F/Gas Mark 4.

2. **Place the flour and** butter in a food processor and blend top a breadcrumb consistency.

3. **Beat the eggs, icing** sugar and vanilla extract together in a bowl and add this into the food processor. Pulse until the ingredients have combined together to form a ball. Do not over work. Remove from the food processor bowl and wrap in cling film. Leave to rest in the fridge for 1 hour, then remove.

5. **On a lightly floured** surface, roll the pastry out to 5mm thick and use it to line a greased 25cm tart ring. Cover with baking parchment, fill with baking beans and bake 'blind' for 20 minutes. Remove from the oven, discard the baking beans and turn down the heat to 150 ° C/300 ° F/Gas Mark 2.

7. **In a saucepan, bring** the whipping cream to the boil with the split vanilla pod. Whisk together the egg yolks and caster sugar before pouring the cream onto them, stirring continually. Pass through a sieve and add a small amount of grated nutmeg.

8. **Pour the mix into** the tart shell and bake on the middle shelf of the over for 30 - 40 minutes or until the custard appears set but not too firm. Turn the tart out onto a plate and serve.

DARK CHOCOLATE GANACHE TART

Metric	Ingredient	Imperial
	3 tbsp slivered blanched almonds	
	6 tbsp sugar	
150 g	(spooned and leveled) all-purpose flour	1 1/4 cups
	2 tsp grated orange or lemon zest	
	1/4 tsp salt	
	6 tbsp unsalted butter, cold and cut into pieces	
340 g	bittersweet chocolate, coarsely chopped	12 oz
150 g	heavy cream	1 1/4 cups
	1 tsp vanilla extract	

Method

1. **Preheat oven to 180** ° C/350 ° F/Gas Mark 4. Make dough: In a food processor, pulse almonds until finely ground. Add sugar, flour, zest (if desired), and salt; pulse until combined. Add butter, pulsing until coarse crumbs form with no large butter lumps (dough should clump together when squeezed with fingers).

2. **Immediately transfer dough to** a 9-inch tart pan with a removable bottom. Using a measuring cup, evenly press dough in bottom and up sides of pan.

3. **Bake in center of** oven until golden brown and firm to the touch, about 20 minutes. Transfer to a wire rack to cool completely, about 1 hour.

4. **Make ganache: Place chocolate** in a large mixing bowl. In a small saucepan, bring cream to a boil. Pour hot cream, through a sieve, over chocolate. Stir until smooth and creamy in texture. Mix in vanilla.

5. **Pour chocolate mixture into** center of cooled tart shell (if chocolate is lumpy, pass through a sieve). Let stand until set, about 2 hours, or chill for 1 hour.

EGG TARTS

Metric	Ingredient	Imperial
	(for the tart pastry)	
120 g	butter, chilled	4 oz
50 g	icing sugar	1 3/4 oz
	1 egg, beaten	
200 g	all purpose flour, sifted	7 oz
	1/2 tsp vanilla essence	
	(for the egg custard)	
500 ml	milk	17 fl oz
140 g	sugar	5 oz
	3 eggs	
	1/2 tsp vanilla essence	

Method

1. **Beat the butter &** icing sugar till well mixed. Add egg & vanilla essence & mix well.

2. **Add flour & mix** into a dough. Cover it in a bowl & let it rest in the fridge for 10 minutes.

3. **Form small dough balls** & roll flat on a floured surface & press into tart moulds or aluminium tart trays.

4. **Bake tart shells for** 10 minutes at 180 degrees celcius. (Tart shells will be half-baked.)

5. **Heat sugar & milk** in a saucepan. Remove from heat once the sugar dissolves.

6. **Whisk eggs slightly (not** till frothy) & pour into the milk mixture. Stir in the vanilla essence.

7. **Strain the egg custard** & pour into the tart shells. Bake at the lower shelf at 180 ° C/350 ° F/Gas Mark 4 for 30 minutes or till the custards firm up.

EMPANADA GALLEGA

Metric	Ingredient (for the pastry)	Imperial	Metric	Ingredient (for the filling)	Imperial
450 g	Flour	1 lb	1 1/2 kg	Chicken, cut into pieces	3 lb
	1 tsp Salt			1 Onion, quartered	
	1/4 tsp Ground cloves			1 tsp Peppercorns	
75 ml	Olive oil	3 fl oz	50 ml	Olive oil	2 fl oz
175 ml	Cold water	6 fl oz		1 Leek, white only, chopped	
	1 Egg white, beaten with 2 tbsp milk			2 Garlic cloves, crushed	
				1 Green pepper, finely chopped	
			125 g	Serrano ham, chopped	4 oz
				4 Tomatoes, blanched, peeled, seeded and chopped	

Method

1. **First make the filling.** Put the chicken into a large saucepan and just cover with water. Add the onion and peppercorns and bring to the boil, skimming off any scum which rises to the surface. Reduce the heat to low, cover the pan and simmer the chicken for 1 hour, or until it is cooked through and tender. Remove the chicken from the pan and set aside until it is cool enough to handle. Discard the cooking liquid and flavourings.

3. **To make the pastry,** sift the flour, salt and cloves into a large bowl. Make a well and pour over the oil and water. Gradually incorporate the flour into the liquid, beating until it comes away from the sides of the bowl. Turn the dough out on to a lightly floured surface and knead lightly until it is smooth and elastic. Cover with a damp cloth and set aside in the refrigerator for 30 minutes.

4. **Cut the chicken into** bite-sized pieces and discard any bones or skin. Heat the oil in a large, deep frying-pan. Add the leek, garlic and pepper and fry until they are soft. Stir in the ham, tomatoes and chicken and cook for 5 minutes, stirring constantly. Remove the pan from the heat. Preheat the oven to moderately hot 190 ° C/375 ° F/ Gas Mark 5.

7. **Divide the dough in** half. On the lightly floured surface, roll out each half to a 23 cm (9 in) circle. Carefully transfer one half to a well-greased baking sheet. Arrange the filling in the centre of the circle, leaving at least a a 2 1/2 cm (1 in) edge all the way round. Using a rolling pin, arrange the second dough circle over the filling. Roll up the edges and crimp them to seal. Cut a deep slit in the centre of the top dough circle. Brush the top and sides of the dough with the egg white mixture and put the baking sheet into the oven. Bake for 30 to 40 minutes, or until the pie is golden brown.

8. **Remove from the oven** and transfer the pie to a warmed serving dish. Serve at once.

FESTIVE MINCE PIES

Metric	Ingredient	Imperial
225 g	cold butter, diced	1/2 lb
350 g	plain flour	12 oz
100 g	golden caster sugar	3 1/2 oz
280 g	mincemeat	10 oz
	1 small egg, beaten	
	icing sugar, to dust	

Method

1. **To make the pastry,** rub the butter into the flour, then mix in the sugar and a pinch of salt. Combine the pastry into a ball - don't add liquid - and knead it briefly. The dough will be fairly firm, like shortbread dough. You can use the dough immediately, or chill for later.

2. **Preheat the oven to** 200 ° C/400 ° F/Gas Mark 6. Line 18 holes of two 12-hole patty tins, by pressing small walnut-sized balls of pastry into each hole. Spoon the mincemeat into the pies.

3. **Take slightly smaller balls** of pastry than before and pat them out between your hands to make round lids, big enough to cover the pies. Top the pies with their lids, pressing the edges gently together to seal - you don't need to seal them with milk or egg as they will stick on their own. (The pies may now be frozen for up to 1 month).

4. **Brush the tops of** the pies with the beaten egg. Bake for 20 minutes until golden. Leave to cool in the tin for 5 minutes, then remove to a wire rack. To serve, lightly dust with icing sugar. They will keep for 3 to 4 days in an airtight container.

FESTIVE NAPOLEON TART

Metric	Ingredient	Imperial
	17 1/2 Frozen puff pastry sheets	
236 ml	Cold milk	1 cup
236 ml	Sour cream	1 cup
	1 package Jello instant pudding, any -flavor, 4 serv.size	

Method

1. **Thaw pastry as directed** on package. Prehaeat oven to 375. Unfold pastry. Cut each sheet into 4 squares. Fold each square in half diagonally. Cut along 2 unfolded edges, leaving 12 in. rim all around and do not cut through to center.

2. **Unfold pastry. Fold outer** top righthand corner over to inner bottom lefthand corner. Fold outer bottom lefthand corner over to inner top righthand corner. Repeat with remaining squares.

3. **Place pastries on baking** sheets. Pierce bottom of each pastry in several places with fork. Bake for 12 to 15 minutes or until golden. If pastry rises in center gently press sown with fork. Cool on rack.

4. **Mix milk and sour** cream in small bowl until smooth. Add pudding mix. Beat with wire whisk until well blwnded, 1 to 2 minutes. Let stand 5 minutes or until slighyly thickened.

5. **Spoon 1 tbsp. Quick** Chocolate Sauce onto bottom of each tart shell. Spoon pudding mixture into shells. Drizzle each tart with 1 tsp, chocolate sauce in stripes.

6. **Pull toothpick through stripes** in up and down motion to feather lines. Chill until ready to serve.

FRANGIPANE TARTLET

Metric	Ingredient	Imperial
400 g	sweet shortcrust pastry	14 oz
	4 balls frozen lemon curd, to serve	
	(for the frangipane)	
120 g	unsalted butter, softened	4 oz
120 g	icing sugar	4 oz
	5 large eggs, beaten	
120 g	ground almonds	4 oz
25 g	plain flour	3/4 oz
	4 tsp dark rum	
	2 tbsp strawberry jam	
	(for the balsamic-marinated strawberries)	
400 g	strawberries, hulled, washed and dried	14 oz
70 g	caster sugar	2 1/2 oz
75 ml	balsamic vinegar	2 1/2 fl oz

Method

1. **Roll out the shortcrust** pastry to 3mm thickness. Cut out 4 discs, using a 10cm circular pastry cutter. Use the pastry discs to line 4 10cm tartlet tins. Place the lined tins on a baking sheet and refrigerate for 20 minutes.

2. **Meanwhile, make the frangipane.** Cream the softened butter with the icing sugar in a mixing bowl until thoroughly mixed. Gradually mix in the beaten egg. Sift the ground almonds and flour and fold them into the butter mixture, then stir in the rum.

3. **Preheat the oven to** 170 º C/325 º F/Gas Mark 3. Brush the chilled pastry cases with strawberry jam. Spread a 0.5cm thick layer of frangipane over the jam. Bake the tartlets for 40 minutes until golden brown.

4. **After the tartlets have** been baking for 30 minutes, prepare the balsamic-marinated strawberries. Place the caster sugar and balsamic vinegar in a saucepan and bring to the boil. Reduce the heat, add the strawberries and warm them gently.

5. **Remove the strawberries from** the balsamic marinade using a slotted spoon. Place the warm strawberries on top of the freshly-baked frangipane tartlets. Top each tartlet with a ball of lemon curd. Serve at once.

GRAPE TART

Metric	Ingredient	Imperial
256 g	all-purpose flour	2 cups
128 g	granulated sugar, divided use	1 cup
64 g	unsalted butter	1/2 cup
	1 large egg	
	1 large egg yolk	
	1 lemon, finely grated, divided use	
	1/8 tsp salt	
	3 large egg whites	
	1/4 tsp cream of tartar	
32 g	finely ground almonds	1/4 cup
450 g	seedless grapes, rinsed, patted dry and halved	1 lb

Method

1. **For the Dough: Sift** flour and 2/3 cup sugar into a medium-size mixing bowl. Cut in butter with a fork until the mixture resembles coarse crumbs. Add egg, egg yolk, half the lemon peel and salt; mix to form a soft dough. Cover the dough with plastic wrap and refrigerate for 20 minutes.

2. **Preheat oven to 180** ° C/350 ° F/Gas Mark 4.

3. **Roll out chilled dough** into a 12-inch circle; place in an ungreased 10-inch springform pan folding the edge down to form a 1-inch high rim (pinch and pat as necessary to create an even edge). Prick crust all over with a fork before baking. Bake crust for 10 minutes; remove from oven and let cool.

4. **For the filling: Beat** egg whites in a medium mixing bowl until stiff and glossy, gradually adding remaining 1/3 cup sugar and cream of tartar while beating. Fold in almonds and remaining lemon peel until well combined; then fold in grapes halves. Spoon evenly into crust and bake for another 30 minutes.

5. **Remove from oven, let** cool for 5 minutes, then remove from pan and cool on a wire rack. Refrigerate, covered with plastic wrap, for an hour before serving.

IRISH BEEF HAND PIES

Metric	Ingredient	Imperial
	1 tbsp vegetable oil	
	1/4 head green cabbage, shredded	
226 g	red potatoes, scrubbed and diced	1/2 lb
454 g	ground beef sirloin	1 lb
	3 tbsp tomato paste	
	1/2 tsp Worcestershire sauce	
	1/2 tsp dried thyme	
	Coarse salt and ground pepper	
	All-purpose flour, for rolling	
	2 piecrusts (9 inches each), homemade or store-bought	

Method

1. Preheat oven to 200 ° C/400 ° F/Gas Mark 6. In a medium saucepan, heat oil over medium; add cabbage and potatoes. Cook until beginning to brown, 7 to 9 minutes. Add beef; cook, breaking up meat with a spoon, until no longer pink, about 5 minutes. Stir in tomato paste, Worcestershire, thyme, and 1 cup water. Cover, and cook until potatoes are tender, about 15 minutes. Lightly mash mixture with a fork. Season with salt and pepper. Let cool completely.

2. On a lightly floured work surface, roll each crust into a 14-inch square; cut each into 4 equal squares. Place 1/2 cup filling on one half of each square, leaving a 1/2-inch border around the filling. Brush borders with water; fold dough over filling to enclose. Crimp edges with a fork to seal. With a paring knife or scissors, cut 3 small vents in each.

3. Transfer pies to 2 foil-lined rimmed baking sheets; bake until golden brown, 10 to 12 minutes, rotating sheets halfway through.

4. To Freeze: Prepare through step 2. Arrange unbaked pies on a baking sheet (they should not touch); freeze until firm, about 1 hour. Wrap each pie in foil. Place in a resealable plastic bag; freeze up to 2 months.

5. To Bake from Frozen: Proceed with step 3, increasing baking time to 28 to 30 minutes.

ITALIAN FRUIT TART

Metric	Ingredient	Imperial
170 g	flour	1 1/3 cups
	2 egg yolks	
64 g	sugar	1/2 cup
64 g	unsalted butter	1/2 cup
	zest from 1 lemon	
128 g	jam	1 cup

Method

1. **Starting with the crust,** sift the flour and sugar into a bowl. Using the pastry blender or two knives cut the butter into the dry ingredients and lemon zest as quickly as possible until the mixture resembles coarse meal.

2. **Add the eggs and** combine them with the other ingredients. Wrap the dough with plastic wrap and refrigerate for 1 hour.

3. **Remove from refrigerator, roll** 2/3 of the dough and place it into a buttered 9 inch tart pan with removable bottom or in a springform pan. Trim all around, fold the overhang under to form the edge and pinch it with your fingertips.

4. **Cover the crust with** abut one cup jam.

5. **Cut the remaining dough** into strips about 1/2 to 3/4 inch wide. Lay the strips of across the top, two or three vertically and horizontally.

6. **Place the crostata in a** preheated oven at 180 ° C/350 ° F/Gas Mark 4 for 30 minutes or until the crust starts to get golden brown.

7. **Let it cool and** serve.

JAM TART

Metric	Ingredient	Imperial
100 g	plain flour	4 oz
	pinch of salt	
50 g	butter or margarine	2 oz
	1 - 2 tbsp water	
100 g	strawberry jam	4 oz

Method

1. **Sift the flour and** salt into a bowl. Rub in the butter or margarine until the mixture resembles fine breadcrumbs.

2. **Stir in just enough** water to bind the ingredients, and lightly mix together. Roll out the pastry on a lightly floured surface, then cut out (2 1/2 in) rounds.

3. **Use these to line** patty tins. Put a small spoonful of jam into each tart. Bake in a moderate oven (200 ° C/400 ° F/Gas Mark 6) for 10 - 15 minutes or until the pastry is golden. Cool on a wire rack. Serve warm or cold.

KEY LIME PIE

Metric	Ingredient	Imperial
200 g	chocolate digestive biscuits	7 oz
50 g	butter, melted	1 3/4 oz
325 g	can condensed milk	11 1/2 oz
	1 egg	
	5 limes, grated zest of 3 limes and juice of 5	
	1 lemon, juice only	
	ice cream, to serve	

Method

1. **Preheat the oven to** 200 ° C/400 ° F/Gas Mark 6. To make the pie base, pop the biscuits into a roomy plastic bag and secure at one end. Crush, with a rolling pin, until they resemble crumbs. Transfer the crumbs to a mixing bowl and add the melted butter. Stir well to combine.

2. **Tip the crumbs into** the base of a 22cm loose-bottomed cake tin, pressing down well with your hand.

3. **Lightly whisk the condensed** milk with the egg. Stir in the lime zest from 2 limes along with the lime and lemon juice.

4. **Pour this mixture onto** the biscuit base in the cake tin. Scatter over the remaining lime zest.

5. **Bake the pie for** about 10 minutes, until just beginning to firm-up. Cool slightly before chilling in the fridge.

6. **Remove the pie from** its tin and serve with ice cream.

LAYERED FRUIT TART

Metric	Ingredient	Imperial
256 g	all-purpose flour	2 cups
128 g	granulated sugar	1 cup
64 g	butter or margarine, softened	1/2 cup
	1 tsp freshly grated lemon peel	
	1 tsp fresh lemon juice	
	1 tsp vanilla	
	3 eggs	
64 g	apricot preserves	1/2 cup
64 g	raspberry preserves	1/2 cup
	1 tbsp amaretto or 1/2 tsp almond extract	
512 g	fresh fruit, such as sliced apple, pear, banana, kiwifruit, figs, raspberries, blackberries, blueberries	4 cups
	1 tsp honey	

Method

1. **Mix flour, granulated sugar,** butter, lemon peel, lemon juice, vanilla and eggs in medium bowl with spoon until dough forms. Place dough on lightly floured surface. Knead about 3 minutes or until dough holds together and is pliable. Shape dough into a ball. Cover with plastic wrap and refrigerate about 20 minutes or until firm.

2. **Heat oven to 180** ° C/350 ° F/Gas Mark 4. Grease pan with butter; lightly flour 11-inch round tart pan with removable bottom or 12-inch pizza pan. Pat dough evenly in pan. Bake about 35 minutes or until toothpick inserted in center comes out clean. Cool completely in pan on wire rack, about 30 minutes.

3. **Heat apricot and raspberry** preserves in 1-quart saucepan over low heat, stirring frequently, until melted. Stir in amaretto. Spread over crust. Arrange fresh fruit on top. Drizzle with honey; sprinkle with powdered sugar. Serve immediately, or cover and refrigerate.

MINI QUICHE OF TUNA

Metric	Ingredient	Imperial
	1 pkg (12) frozen mini tarts	
	1 can tuna liquid removed, flaked	
32 g	Swiss cheese, grated	1/4 cup
32 g	Cheddar cheese, grated	1/4 cup
	2 tbsp grated onion	
	1/2 (6 ounce.) pkg. frzn Spinach, cooked, liquid removed, and minced	
	2 Large eggs	
64 g	table cream	1/2 cup
	Salt	
	Freshly ground pepper	
	1/2 tsp nutmeg	

Method

1. **Preheat the oven to** 180 ° C/350 ° F/Gas Mark 4.

2. **Coat the inside, bottom,** and sides of the frozen tart shells with beaten egg white.

3. **Bake for 5 minutes.**

4. **Remove from the oven** and divide the tuna into each tart shell.

5. **Add in grated cheeses,** then onion and minced spinach.

6. **Whisk Large eggs in** bowl. Add in the cream and whisk until lemon colored.

7. **Flavor with salt, pepper,** and nutmeg. Pour the egg mix into the tart shells to the top and then bake for 30-40 min until the centers are cooked. Can be made with smaller tarts.

MINI QUICHE OF VEGETABLES

Metric	Ingredient	Imperial
	1 package (15 oz/425 g) refrigerated pie crusts (2 crusts)	
118 ml	milk	1/2 cup
	2 eggs	
	4 slices bacon, crisply cooked, drained and chopped	
128 g	finely chopped zucchini	1/2 cup
128 g	finely chopped mushrooms	1/2 cup
	1 green onion with top, sliced	
56 g	shredded cheddar cheese	2 ounces
	1 garlic clove, pressed	
	Dash of ground black pepper	

Method

1. **Preheat oven to 190** ° C/375 ° F/Gas Mark 5. Let pie crusts stand at room temperature 15 minutes. Lightly spray Muffin Pan with vegetable oil. Whisk milk and eggs.

2. **Chop bacon, zucchini and** mushrooms. Add bacon, zucchini, mushrooms, green onion, cheese, pressed garlic and black pepper to mixing bowl; set aside.

3. **On lightly floured surface,** roll one crust to a 12-inch circle. Using a Scalloped Bread Tube, cut out 12 pastry pieces. Press one pastry piece into each muffin cup. Repeat with remaining crust to fill remaining muffin cups.

4. **Fill each muffin cup** with a rounded scoop of vegetable mixture. Bake 17-20 minutes or until crusts are light golden brown. Cool in pan 2 minutes; carefully remove mini quiches from pan. Serve warm.

PEACH PIE

Metric	Ingredient	Imperial
	3 Egg Whites	
128 g	Granulated Sugar	1 cup
	14 Saltine Crackers, finely crushed	
	1 tsp Vanilla Extract	
	1/4 tsp Baking Powder	
64 g	Pecans, chopped	1/2 cup
	7 Fresh Peaches, peeled, pitted and sliced	
256 g	Sweetened Whipped Cream	2 cups

Method

1. **Preheat the oven to** 170 ° C/325 ° F/Gas Mark 3.

2. **Whip the egg whites** in a large glass bowl until they hold a stiff peak. Sprinkle the sugar in gradually, continually whipping the egg whites.

3. **Fold in the crushed** saltine crackers, pecans, baking powder and vanilla.

4. **Spread the mixture evenly** into an ungreased 9 inch deep dish pie plate. Bake for 30 minutes, or until a toothpick inserted into the center comes out clean.

5. **Remove the pie from** the oven and allow to cool completely.

6. **When the crust has** cooled completely, place the sliced peaches evenly over the top.

7. **Cover the pie with** aluminum foil to avoid browning.

8. **When ready to serve,** evenly top with whipped cream.

PECAN TART

Metric	Ingredient	Imperial
225 g	Shortcrust Pastry	8 oz
50 g	pecan nuts	2 oz
	3 eggs	
225 g	golden (light corn) syrup	8 oz
75 g	soft brown sugar	3 oz
	2.5 ml vanilla essence (extract)	
	A pinch of salt	

Method

1. **Roll out the pastry** (paste) on a lightly floured surface and use to line a greased 23 cm/9 in flan dish.

2. **Cover with greaseproof (waxed)** paper, fill with baking beans and bake blind in a preheated oven at 190 ° C/375 ° F/ Gas Mark 5 for 10 minutes. Remove the paper and beans.

3. **Arrange the pecans in** an attractive pattern in the pastry case (pie shell). Beat the eggs until light and frothy. Beat in the syrup, then the sugar and continue beating until the sugar has dissolved. Add the vanilla essence and salt and beat until smooth.

4. **Spoon the mixture into** the case and bake in the preheated oven for 10 minutes.

5. **Reduce the oven temperature** to 180 ° C/350 ° F/Gas Mark 4 and bake for a further 30 minutes until golden. Leave to cool and set before serving.

PIZZA

Metric	Ingredient	Imperial	Metric	Ingredient	Imperial
	(for the Pizza Dough)			2 tbsp tomato puree	
175 g	strong white flour	6 oz		2 tbsp chopped fresh mixed herbs	
	1/2 tsp salt			(for the final topping)	
	1 tsp easy dried yeast			8 slices of pepperoni sausage	
120 ml	lukewarm water	4 fl oz	125 g	grated mature Cheddar cheese	4 1/2 oz
	2 tbsp olive oil		125 g	fresh parmesan	4 1/2 oz
	(for the tomato sauce)			6 fresh Basil leaves	
	2 tbsp olive oil				
	1 medium onion				
	1 garlic clove (optional)				
400 g	can chopped tomatoes	14 oz			

Method

1. Sieve the flour and salt over a large bowl. Stir in the yeast and then a well in the centre of the dry ingredients. Pour in the water and oil and mix well.

2. When a soft dough has formed, knead the dough on a lightly floured board for 10 mins. When the dough has become elastic-like, place in a lightly greased bowl, cover with clingfilm and leave in a warm place for about an hour.

3. Turn the dough then onto the board again and knead for a further 2 mins. Roll out into a circle, about 1/4" thick (thicker if you prefer a slightly more deep pan style pizza) and "knock" the edge up a little to give the pizza a rim.

4. Heat the oil in a saucepan, add in the finely chopped onion, crushed garlic and gently fry for 5 mins. Add the tomatoes, tomato puree, herbs, sugar and seasoning.

5. Simmer uncovered, stirring occasionally for 20 mins or until the tomatoes have reduced to a thick pulp. Leave to cool.

6. Place the pizza base onto a pizza tray or baking tray and carefully spoon the tomato sauce onto the pizza base and smooth over the surface.

7. Add half of the grated cheese, place the pepperoni pizza around the top, sprinkle over the rest of both the cheeses. Tear the basil leaves and pop on the top to add that extra bit of colour.

8. Cook in the oven on 220 ° C/425 ° F/Gas Mark 7 for 12 minutes or until golden brown.

POT PIE WITH LIVER

Metric	Ingredient	Imperial
	Pastry for two crust pie	
64 g	Minced onion	1/2 cup
	6 tbsp Butter	
	1 tsp Salt	
64 g	All purpose flour	1/2 cup
710 ml	Chicken broth	3 cups
384 g	Cubed cooked chicken livers	3 cups
64 g	Cooked peas	1/2 cup
64 g	Cooked carrots (finely diced)	1/2 cup
32 g	Minced pimientos	1/4 cup

Method

1. **Prepare the pastry; rollout** to 1/4 inch thick. Cut to fit the tops of six individual casseroles.

2. **Bake on an ungreased** baking sheet at 230 º C/450 º F/Gas Mark 8 for 10 to 12 min. Meanwhile, cook onion in butter till tender but not brown.

3. **Blend in flour and** salt. Cook, stirring constantly till flour is cooked. Add in broth all at one time. Cook and stir till thick and bubbly; add in remaining ingredients. Heat until bubbling.

4. **Pour into 6 heated** individual casseroles. Place pastry on warm filling just before serving.

POTATO MEAT PIE

Metric	Ingredient	Imperial
450 g	ground beef	1 lb
330 g	instant potato flakes	2 2/3 cups
	1 egg	
	1 tsp salt	
	1/8 tsp pepper	
	1 minced onion	
32 g	ketchup	1/4 cup
236 ml	milk	1 cup
16 g	margarine	1/8 cup
64 g	shredded cheese	1/2 cup

Method

1. **Mix beef,** 1 1/3 cup dry potato flakes, egg, 1/2 tsp salt, pepper, onion, ketchup, and 1/2 cup milk.

2. **Place in 2 loaf** pans. Bake 180 ° C/350 ° F/Gas Mark 4.

3. **Boil** 1 1/3 **cups** water with 1/8 cup margarine and 1/2 tsp salt. Remove from heat and add 1/2 cup milk to boiling water.

4. **Stir in** 1 1/3 cups dry instant potato flakes. Spread on top of meatloaf. Top with shredded cheese.

5. **Return to oven until** cheese is melted.

PUMPKIN PIE

Metric	Ingredient	Imperial
	1 package cream cheese, softened	
256 g	canned pumpkin, mashed	2 cups
128 g	sugar	1 cup
	1/4 tsp salt	
	1 egg plus 2 egg yolks, slightly beaten	
128 g	half-and-half	1 cup
32 g	melted butter	1/4 cup
	1 tsp vanilla extract	
	1/2 tsp ground cinnamon	
	1/4 tsp ground ginger, optional	
	1 piece pre-made pie dough	
	Whipped cream, for topping	

Method

1. Preheat the oven to 180 ° C/350 ° F/Gas Mark 4.

2. Place 1 piece of pre-made pie dough down into a (9-inch) pie pan and press down along the bottom and all sides. Pinch and crimp the edges together to make a pretty pattern. Put the pie shell back into the freezer for 1 hour to firm up.

3. Fit a piece of aluminum foil to cover the inside of the shell completely. Fill the shell up to the edges with pie weights or dried beans (about 2 pounds) and place it in the oven. Bake for 10 minutes, remove the foil and pie weights and bake for another 10 minutes or until the crust is dried out and beginning to color.

4. For the filling, in a large mixing bowl, beat the cream cheese with a hand mixer. Add the pumpkin and beat until combined. Add the sugar and salt, and beat until combined. Add the eggs mixed with the yolks, half-and-half, and melted butter, and beat until combined. Finally, add the vanilla, cinnamon, and ginger, if using, and beat until incorporated.

5. Pour the filling into the warm prepared pie crust and bake for 50 minutes, or until the center is set. Place the pie on a wire rack and cool to room temperature. Cut into slices and top each piece with a generous amount of whipped cream.

RASPBERRY TARTLET

Metric	Ingredient	Imperial
	(for the pastry)	
128 g	flour	1 cup
113 g	cream cheese, softened	4 oz
64 g	butter, softened	1/2 cup
	1/4 teaspoon salt	
	(for the cream cheese filling)	
226 g	cream cheese, softened	8 oz
64 g	powdered sugar	1/2 cup
	1 tbsp fresh lemon juice	
320 g	fresh raspberries	2 1/2 cups
64 g	red currant jelly	1/2 cup

Method

1. Using an electric mixer, mix together flour, cream cheese, butter, and salt until a dough forms. Wrap the dough in plastic and refrigerate at least 30 minutes (or up to 24 hours). If chilled longer than 1 hour, let the dough warm up at room temperature for about 20 minutes.

2. Divide the dough into 10 balls and place them in a standard size muffin pan. Press each dough ball into the bottom and up the sides of the muffin cup to form a shell.

3. Bake at 180 ° C/350 ° F/Gas Mark 4 until nicely browned, about 20-25 minutes. Carefully invert the pan to the remove baked shells, and cool on a wire rack.

4. With an electric mixer, beat the cream cheese with the powdered sugar until smooth. Beat in the lemon juice. Spread a heaping tablespoon of the cream cheese mixture on the bottom of each cooled pastry shell. Arrange the berries on top.

5. For a more formal presentation, just before serving, heat 1/2 cup red currant jelly in a small saucepan and use a pastry brush to glaze berries with the warm jelly.

6. Refrigerate until ready to serve. The tartlets will keep for several days in the refrigerator.

RHUBARB AND CUSTARD CRUMBLE TART

Metric	Ingredient	Imperial
350 g	rhubarb	12 oz
100 g	golden caster sugar	3 1/2 oz
350 g	sweet shortcrust pastry	12 oz
	1 large egg and 1 egg yolk	
	1 tsp vanilla extract	
	1 tbsp plain flour	
284 ml	carton single cream	9 1/2 fl oz
	(for the crumble topping)	
50 g	butter, melted	1 3/4 oz
50 g	demerara sugar	1 3/4 oz
50 g	porridge oats	1 3/4 oz
	1/2 tsp ground ginger	

Method

1. Cut the rhubarb into bite-size pieces, then put them in a frying pan with half the sugar and warm through just until the sugar dissolves. Immediately tip the rhubarb into a bowl with the juices and leave to cool. Preheat the oven to 180 ° C/350 ° F/Gas Mark 4.

2. Roll out the pastry quite thinly and use to line a deep, loose-based 24cm fluted flan tin. Line with greaseproof paper and baking beans and bake for about 20 minutes until the pastry is pale golden and no longer raw.

3. Beat together the egg and egg yolk, vanilla extract, remaining caster sugar and the flour. Gradually whisk in the cream with any juice from the rhubarb (you should have a tablespoonful or two). Now spoon the rhubarb into the prepared pastry case and pour the cream mixture over.

4. Turn the oven temperature up to 200 ° C/400 ° F/Gas Mark 6 and bake for about 20 minutes, or until the custard is very lightly set and there is a thin skin on the top.

5. Mix together all the topping ingredients and spoon evenly over the pie. Return it to the oven for a further 15 minutes or until the crumble is golden and the custard set with just a little wobble. The top of the pie may have risen and cracked when you take it from the oven but don't worry as it will settle back again on cooling. Serve warm.

RHUBARB PIE

Metric	Ingredient	Imperial
	(for the pastry)	
225 g	butter	8 oz
55 g	caster sugar	2 oz
	2 eggs, preferably free range	
340 g	white flour, preferably unbleached	12 oz
	(for the filling)	
750 g	red rhubarb, sliced about 1cm(1/2in) thick	1 1/2 lb
250-400 g	sugar	9oz-14 oz

Method

1. **Preheat the oven to** 180 ° C/350 ° F/Gas Mark 4.

2. **First make the pastry.** Cream the butter and sugar together by hand or in a food mixer (no need to over cream).

3. **Add the eggs and** beat for several minutes. Reduce speed and mix in the flour.

4. **Turn out onto a** piece of floured greaseproof paper, flatten into a round wrap and chill. This pastry needs to be chilled for at least 1 hour otherwise it is difficult to handle.

5. **To make the tart,** roll out the pastry 3mm/1/8in thick approximately and use about 2/3rds of it to line a 21.5cm/8 3/4in square x 2.5cm/1in deep with fluted edge tin.

6. **Lay the rhubarb in** the pastry base and sprinkle with the sugar.

7. **Cover with a lid** of pastry, seal edges, decorate with pastry leaves, brush with the egg wash and bake in the preheated oven until the rhubarb is tender, approximately 45 minutes to 1 hour (but do keep checking some ovens may vary cooking time).

RICOTTA AND PROSCUITTO TART

Metric	Ingredient	Imperial	Metric	Ingredient	Imperial
880 ml	whole-milk ricotta cheese	30 fl oz		1/8 tsp freshly ground black pepper	
256 g	all-purpose flour	2 cups		1/2 cup peeled and diced onion	
	1 tsp kosher salt			1 1/2 tsp minced fresh marjoram	
	12 tbsp butter, cut into 1/2-inch pieces and chilled		113 g	prosciutto, diced	1/4 lb
	5 tbsp ice water			3 large eggs	
	2 tbsp olive oil			1/8 tsp freshly grated nutmeg	
453 g	spinach, stemmed and cleaned	1 lb			

Method

1. **Place the ricotta in** a strainer lined with cheesecloth and allow to drain over a bowl, covered and refrigerated, for 2 hours.

2. **To prepare the tart** dough, combine the flour and 1/2 teaspoon of the salt in a bowl. Add the chilled butter and blend until the mixture resembles coarse meal. Work in the ice water until the dough holds together. Form the dough into a smooth, flat disk, wrap in plastic, and refrigerate for at least 1 hour. Lightly flour a work surface and roll the dough into a 16 inch disk. Place the rolled-out dough into a 10 x 2 1/2 -inch-deep cake pan or springform mold. Pressing with your fingertips, flute the top edges of the dough. Place in the freezer and chill thoroughly, about 30 minutes.

3. **In a medium skillet,** heat 1 tbsp of olive oil over high heat and saute the spinach, stirring for about 2 minutes. Season with 1/4 teaspoon salt and half the pepper. Place the cooked spinach in a colander and drain. Chop fine and reserve.In the same skillet, add the remaining tbsp olive oil and cook the onion 3 to 5 minutes over medium heat until translucent. Add the marjoram and prosciutto. Stir and cook an additional 2 minutes. Set aside.

4. **Preheat the oven to** 220 ° C/425 ° F/Gas Mark 7. In a large bowl, beat the eggs and add the drained ricotta, spinach, onion, and prosciutto. Season with the nutmeg and remaining salt and pepper. Set aside. Line the tart shell with aluminum foil and fill with pastry weights. Bake for 12 to 15 minutes. Remove the foil and weights and cook for 10 minutes, or until the dough is light brown.

5. **Lower the oven temperature** to 190 ° C/375 ° F/Gas Mark 5. Spread the ricotta and spinach mixture evenly in the tart, place on the middle rack of the oven, and bake for 1 hour and 10 minutes, until the filling is set and the top golden brown. Let rest for 15 to 20 minutes, slice into wedges, and serve.

SHEPHERDS PIE

Metric	Ingredient	Imperial
	1 tbsp sunflower oil	
	1 large onion , chopped	
	2-3 medium carrots , chopped	
500 g	minced lamb	1 lb
	2 tbsp tomato purée	
	large splash Worcestershire sauce	
500 ml	beef stock	17 fl oz
900 g	potatoes , cut into chunks	2 lb
85 g	butter	3 oz
	3 tbsp milk	

Method

1. **Heat the oil in** a medium saucepan, then soften the onion and carrots for a few mins. When soft, turn up the heat, crumble in the lamb and brown, tipping off any excess fat.

2. **Add the tomato purée** and Worcestershire sauce, then fry for a few mins. Pour over the stock, bring to a simmer, then cover and cook for 40 mins, uncovering halfway.

3. **Meanwhile, heat the oven** to 180 ° C/350 ° F/Gas Mark 4, then make the mash. Boil the potatoes in salted water for 10-15 mins until tender. Drain, then mash with the butter and milk.

4. **Put the mince into** an ovenproof dish, top with the mash and ruffle with a fork. The pie can now be chilled and frozen for up to a month. Bake for 20-25 mins until the top is starting to colour and the mince is bubbling through at the edges. (To bake from frozen, cook at 150 ° C/300 ° F/Gas Mark 2 for 1 hr-1 hr 20 mins until piping hot in the centre. Flash under the grill to brown, if you like.) Leave to stand for 5 mins before serving.

SLICED HAM AND EGG PIE

Metric	Ingredient	Imperial
32 g	butter	1/4 cup
32 g	all-purpose flour	1/4 cup
	1/2 tsp salt	
	1/4 tsp ground mustard	
	1/8 tsp pepper	
236 ml	milk	1 cup
	1 tsp dried minced onion	
320 g	fully cooked ham, cubed	2 1/2 cups
128 g	frozen peas, thawed	1 cup
	2 hard-boiled eggs, chopped	
	pastry for single crust pie, 8-inch	

Method

1. **Melt butter in saucepan;** stir in flour, salt mustard and pepper until smooth. Gradually add milk and onion; bring to a boil, stirring constantly.

2. **Continue cooking and stirring** for about 2 minutes longer, until thickened. Stir in ham, peas and hard-cooked eggs.

3. **Pour mixture into an** 8-inch square baking dish. On a floured surface, roll pastry to fit top of dish; place over filling. Seal and crimp edges; cut slits in the top.

4. **Bake at 220 ° C/425 ° F/Gas Mark 7** for 25 minutes or until crust is golden brown and filling is bubbly.

SPINACH AND ARTICHOKE PIE

Metric	Ingredient	Imperial
	2 small leek, very thinly sliced	
50 g	butter, plus a knob	1 3/4 oz
400 g	frozen leaf spinach, thawed and well drained and chopped	14 oz
250 g	ricotta cheese	1/2 lb
	4 large egg, beaten	
140 g	grated parmesan cheese	5 oz
	1/2 nutmeg, grated	
400 g	can artichoke heart, drained and halved	14 oz
85 g	SunBlush tomato	3 oz
270 g	pack filo pastry	9 1/2 oz
	2 tbsp olive oil	

Method

1. **Soften the leeks in** the butter for a couple of mins. Add the spinach to the pan, cover and cook for 5-6 mins more until the spinach has just thawed.

2. **In a separate bowl,** beat the ricotta and eggs with the parmesan, spinach mix, nutmeg and plenty of seasoning. Stir in the artichokes and tomatoes.

3. **Heat oven to 180** ° C/350 ° F/Gas Mark 4. Line the base and sides of a greased 23cm clip-sided or loose-based tin with the filo pastry. Brushing each sheet lightly with the oil, place in the tin, oil-side down, leaving excess to hang over the edge. Turn the tin a quarter turn after each sheet.

4. **Tip filling into the** tin, fold excess pastry onto the top of the pie, a sheet at a time, crumpling to give a ruffled effect. Bake for 11/2hrs until golden and firm.

SPINACH QUICHE TART

Metric	Ingredient	Imperial
	1 box refrigerated pie crusts, softened as directed on box	
	2 slices bacon	
	4 medium green onions, chopped	
	2 eggs	
64 g	half-and-half	1/2 cup
64 g	grated Parmesan cheese	1/2 cup
	1/4 tsp salt	
	1/8 tsp ground nutmeg	
255 g	frozen spinach, thawed and squeezed to drain	9 oz

Method

1. **Heat oven to 190** ° C/375 ° F/Gas Mark 5. Remove pie crusts from package; place flat on work surface. With a 2 1/2-inch round cutter, cut 12 rounds from each crust. Press 1 round in bottom and up side of each of 24 ungreased miniature muffin cups.

2. **Cook bacon in 10** inch skillet over medium heat 4 to 6 minutes, turning occasionally, until brown and crisp. Drain on paper towels. Add onions to same skillet with bacon drippings. Cook 2 to 3 minutes, stirring constantly, until tender; drain.

3. **Beat eggs, half-and-half, cheese,** salt and nutmeg in medium bowl with wire whisk. Crumble bacon; add to egg mixture. Add onions and spinach; mix well. Divide mixture evenly among pie crust lined cups.

4. **Bake spinach quiche tarts** 20 to 25 minutes or until puffed and golden brown. Cool in pan on wire rack 10 minutes. Loosen and remove quiches from pan with tip of knife. Serve warm or cool. Store in refrigerator.

STEAK AND KIDNEY PIE

Metric	Ingredient	Imperial	Metric	Ingredient	Imperial
	2 tbsp plain flour			(for the 'rough puff' pastry)	
	black pepper		500 g	strong bread flour	1 lb
700 g	lean stewing beef, or chuck steak	1 1/2 lb		1/2 tsp salt	
225 g	beef kidneys, cut into chunks	8 oz	500 g	butter	1 lb
	1 tbsp vegetable oil		25 ml	cold water	1 fl oz
25 g	butter	1 oz		1 beaten egg, to glaze	
	2 onions, chopped				
	2 bay leaves				
170 ml	stout	5 3/4 fl oz			
400 ml	strong beef stock	13 1/2 fl oz			
	1 tsp gravy, browning				

Method

1. **Season the flour and** toss the steak and kidney in it to coat.

2. **Heat the oil and** butter in a large pan and fry the meat for 5 minutes or until brown. Add the onions and cook for another 3-4 minutes, stirring. Add the bay leaves, stout and stock.

3. **Stir in the gravy** browning and cook for 2-3 minutes, until thickened. Cover and simmer for about 1 hour and 30 minutes, until the meat is tender.

4. **For the pastry, mix** the flour and salt together and gently add the butter. Make a well adding the water and bring lightly together to make a dough. Roll out into a rectangle and mark into thirds. Fold over the end thirds into the centre one, turn through 90° and repeat two more times. Chill for half an hour.

5. **When the meat is** cooked, cool slightly and tip into a pie dish. Roll out the pastry on a floured surface a little bigger than the size of the dish using the trimmings to make a strip the width of the rim.

10. **Brush the rim of** the pie dish with beaten egg and lay the pastry strip on top to make a seal. Brush again with egg and lay the lid on top. Crimp or flute the edges, brush the lid with the remaining egg and make a slit in the top.

11. **Bake at 200** ° C/400 ° F/Gas Mark 6 for about 20 minutes, until golden. Serve with buttered spring cabbage and mashed potato.

STRAWBERRY PIE

Metric	Ingredient	Imperial
	1 (9 inch) pie crust, baked	
1 l	fresh strawberries	1 quart
128 g	white sugar	1 cup
	3 tbsp cornstarch	
96 g	water	3/4 cup
64 g	heavy whipping cream	1/2 cup

Method

1. **Arrange half of strawberries** in baked pastry shell. Mash remaining berries and combine with sugar in a medium saucepan. Place saucepan over medium heat and bring to a boil, stirring frequently.

2. **In a small bowl,** whisk together cornstarch and water.

3. **Gradually stir cornstarch mixture** into boiling strawberry mixture. Reduce heat and simmer mixture until thickened, about 10 minutes, stirring constantly.

4. **Pour mixture over berries** in pastry shell.

5. **Chill for several hours** before serving. In a small bowl, whip cream until soft peaks form. Serve each slice of pie with a dollop of whipped cream.

STRAWBERRY STREUSEL

Metric	Ingredient	Imperial
128 g	plain flour	1 cup
64 g	sugar	1/2 cup
	2 tsp baking powder	
	1/2 tsp salt	
120 ml	milk	1/2 cup
	1 tsp vanilla essence	
	1 egg	
	2 tbsp melted butter	
192 g	strawberries, sliced	1-1/2 cups
	(for the streusel topping)	
32 g	flour	1/4 cup
32 g	sugar	1/4 cup
	2 tbsp butter	
64 g	chopped pecan nuts	1/2 cup

Method

1. **Grease and dust with** flour a 7" round baking pan.

2. **In a medium bowl,** stir together the flour, sugar, baking powder and salt with a whisk.

3. **Make a well in** the middle and add the vanilla essence, the egg and melted butter (make sure it's not hot, or the egg will cook!). Beat this till well mixed.

4. **Pour the batter into** the prepared pan. Level with the back of a wet spoon. Arrange the sliced strawberries on the top, without pressing them into the batter.

5. **In a small bowl,** combine the flour and sugar for the topping. Cut in the butter with two knives, or rub it in with your fingertips till the mixture is the consistency of coarse breadcrumbs.

6. **Mix in the pecan** nuts and sprinkle thickly over the batter.

7. **Bake at 180 °** C/350 ° F/Gas Mark 4 for 35-40 minutes or till the cake is done.

SWEET PLUM TART

Metric	Ingredient	Imperial
	(for the pastry)	
32 g	shortening	1/4 cup
64 g	hot water	1/2 cup
	1/2 tbsp milk	
192 g	all purpose flour	1 1/2 cups
	1/4 tsp salt	
	(for the filling)	
	9 large plums, cut in half and pitted	
43 g	sugar	1/3 cup
	1 tbsp lemon juice	
	1 egg, beaten	
	1 tbsp sugar	
43 g	sliced almonds	1/3 cup

Method

1. **Place shortening in large** bowl. Pour hot water and milk over the shortening.

2. **With a dinner fork,** break up the shortening. Tilt bowl and beat quickly until the mixture looks like whipped cream.

3. **Pour flour and salt** over shortening mixture and beat well with the fork, forming a dough that cleans the bowl.

4. **Roll the pastry out** into 10 inch circle. Fit into a 9" pie pan with removable bottom and chill while preparing plums.

5. **Cut and pit plums.** Mix 1/3 cup sugar with lemon juice and egg and beat well. Place plums cut side down into pastry.

6. **Pour egg mixture over** the plums and sprinkle with 1 tbsp sugar.

7. **Bake at 180 ° C/350 ° F/ Gas Mark 4** for 50-60 minutes, until crust is light golden brown, plums are tender and filling is set.

SWEETHEART PASTRY

Metric	Ingredient	Imperial	Metric	Ingredient	Imperial
	(for the filling)			2 tbsp caster sugar	
250 g	winter melon, strips, candied, chopped	9 oz		1 tbsp golden syrup	
			100 g	shortening	3 1/2 oz
60 g	sesame seeds, toasted	2 oz		1/4 tsp vanilla essence	
65 g	caster sugar	2 oz	150 ml	water	5 fl oz
80 g	glutinous-rice flour, cooked (koh fun)			(for the oil dough)	
120 ml	water	4 fl oz	120 g	plain flour, sifted	4 oz
	2 tbsp oil		100 g	shortening	3 1/2 oz
	(for the water dough)			(for the glaze)	
150 g	high-protein flour, sifted	5 1/3 oz		1 egg, beaten with 1/8 tsp salt	
150 g	plain flour	5 1/3 oz			

Method

1. **Preheat oven at** 180 ° C/350 ° F/Gas Mark 4.

2. **Mix filling ingredients. Divide** into 60g portions.

3. **Mix water dough ingredients.** Set aside for 1/2 hour. Divide into as many pieces as there are filling portions.

4. **Mix flour and shortening.** Place in plastic wrap and place in fridge for 1/2 hour. Divide into portions also.

5. **Wrap oil dough in** water dough. Roll flat into round pieces.

6. **Place filling in dough** and flatten. Brush egg glaze.

7. **Place cakes on greased** cookie sheet and bake at 180C for 20-25 minutes.

TARTES AU CITRON

Metric	Ingredient	Imperial
	(for the pastry)	
150 g	plain flour	5 oz
	Pinch of salt	
100 g	unsalted butter	3 1/2 oz
50 g	caster sugar	1 1/4 oz
	1 medium egg	
	Few drops of vanilla extract	
	(for the filling)	
	3 medium eggs	
100 g	caster sugar	3 1/2 oz
142 ml	carton double cream	
	Finely zested rind and juice of 3 lemons	
	Icing sugar, for dusting	

Method

1. **To make the pastry:** Tip the flour and salt into a bowl, and add the butter, cut into chunks. Rub the butter into the flour until the mixture resembles fine breadcrumbs. Stir in the sugar and then add the egg and vanilla extract, and mix to bind the ingredients together.

2. **Tip the dough out** on to a floured worktop and knead it very lightly to give a smooth surface, then roll it out and use it to line the flan tin. Chill the pastry case for at least 15 minutes. Set the oven to 190 ° C/375 ° F/Gas Mark 5 and place a baking sheet in the oven to heat up.

3. **Line pastry case with** a sheet of baking parchment and fill with baking beans. Bake for 12 minutes, then carefully lift out the parchment paper with the baking beans and return the case to the oven for a further 3-5 minutes, or until light golden. Remove from oven. Reduce oven temperature to 180 ° C/350 ° F/Gas Mark 4.

4. **To make the filling:** Beat the eggs, then add sugar, cream and lemon rind and juice, and mix well. Pour mixture into the pastry case, filling it almost to the top.

5. **Bake the tart in** the centre of the oven for 20-30 minutes, or until the edges of the filling have set and it is just slightly wobbly in the centre. Remove from the oven, slide the flan tin on to a wire rack and leave the tart to cool in the tin for about 20-30 minutes. Remove from the tin and leave to cool completely.

TRADITIONAL MEAT PUFF PASTRY PIE

Metric	Ingredient	Imperial
750 g	lean braising steak	1. 6 lb
	4 tbsp plain flour	
	Freshly ground salt and pepper	
	4 tbsp olive oil	
	1 tbsp tomato purée	
500 ml	Guinness	17 fl oz
350 g	shallots, peeled	12 oz
	Few sprigs of thyme	
	2 bay leaves	
	2 garlic cloves, peeled	
500 g	shortcrust pastry	1 lb
	1 free-range egg yolk mixed with 1 tbsp water	

Method

1. **Dice the beef into** 2.5cm cubes. Place the flour in a medium-sized bowl and season well with salt and pepper. Roll the beef in the flour to coat.

2. **Heat the oil in** a large pan and fry the beef until golden brown in colour. Add the tomato purée and cook for 1 minute, stirring well. Then pour in the Guinness and add the shallot, thyme, bay leaf and garlic. Season with salt and pepper. Cover and simmer for 1 1/2 hours. Remove the bay leaf and discard.

3. **Preheat the oven to** 200 ° C/400 ° F/Gas Mark 6.

4. **Transfer the meat to** a 20cm pie dish 5-7cm deep.

5. **Roll out the pastry** and cover the pie. Scrunch the pastry to the edge of the dish and trim around the edge, leaving 1-2cm overhanging. Brush the top with the egg.

6. **Transfer to a baking** tray and place in the oven. Bake for 15-20 minutes and serve immediately.

TRADITIONAL PORK PIE

Metric	Ingredient	Imperial
	(for the filling)	
450 g	pork shoulder, finely chopped	1 lb
55 g	pork fat, finely minced	2 oz
55 g	bacon, minced	2 oz
	(for the pastry)	
450 g	flour	1 lb
225 g	lard	8 oz
90 ml	water	3 fl oz
	beaten egg yolks, or milk to glaze	
	(for the jelly)	
300 ml	water	10 fl oz
	1/2 envelope powdered gelatine	
	parsley, or other herbs (optional)	

Method

1. **To make the pastry:** put the flour in a mixing bowl and crumble in the lard. Work until beginning to come together. Add a pinch of salt and start adding the water gradually, working until the dough breaks (NB. it must not be stretchable). Let it rest for 1 hour. Preheat the oven to 190 ° C/375 ° F/Gas Mark 5.

3. **Knead the dough on** a floured surface and roll out about 5mm thick. Reserve enough pastry to make a lid. Use the larger piece of dough to line the base and sides of a 20cm plain flan ring or springform tin.

4. **To make the filling:** mix the pork shoulder, pork fat and bacon and season with salt and pepper. Place this mixture in the dough case, but don't squash it in.

5. **Brush the edges of** the dough with water and place the lid on top. Make sure this is sealed well by pressing with a fork. Brush the top with egg yolk or milk. Cook in the oven for about 1 hour 30 minutes until golden brown.

7. **Remove from the oven** and remove the flan ring immediately. Leave the pie to cool, and then chill overnight.

8. **The following day, make** up the gelatine with the water according to the packet instructions. You can add parsley or other herbs if desired. Make a hole in the top of the pie and pour the gelatine in until the pie is completely filled (the meat will have shrunk so there will be plenty of space). Let the pie set in the fridge overnight.